Bonus:
Free
Premium
Theme

2
0
2
2

WORDPRESS IN 10 DAYS

Learn how to build
a professional theme
without knowing PHP

P. A. Gabriel

ISBN: 978-87-999829-7-4

Published by Tech Stuff House, an imprint of Virgo Publishers. contact@virgopublishers.com

To contact the author, email us at authors@virgopublishers.com.

CONTENTS

INTRODUCTION

The WordPress platform powers over 30% of all active websites on the internet. With such a big market, the demand for professionals capable of customizing, maintaining, and creating themes from scratch is very high. Those who already work with website building, but have not yet ventured into the WP area, are missing out on many job opportunities. And it is for these people that I wrote this book.

With a straightforward, step-by-step approach, you can start building a theme right from the first hour of reading by following all the instructions provided. And the best of all is that you don't need to know how to code in PHP because the structure of a WordPress theme is built with HTML. The PHP part is mostly the functions that create all the dynamic content, but it is possible to use them without the knowledge of the language itself. I guarantee it is easier than applying a high school mathematical formula.

To further speed up the learning curve, the theme that we will develop together throughout this book, and which I created as a personal project, is available for download so you can analyze and even reuse the code in your projects.

Learning to work with WordPress has never been easier than it is now. Read all the topics presented here and climb the ladder of your developer career.

When you finish this book, you will be able to develop a theme like this:

CHAPTER 1

Learning Method

In this book, you will learn how to build a professional WP theme using blocks of code used to build the project, followed by relevant explanations of how the code works. Thus, knowledge absorption happens naturally without having to read long texts. Comments will be made in the most direct and simple way possible, without going too deep into the individual concepts, because what matters most is knowing what it is for and how to use a particular piece of code.

Requirements

Inevitably, advanced knowledge of HTML and CSS is necessary to develop a WP theme, as we will extensively use these two languages throughout the project, which aims to eliminate the need to know PHP. If you are already familiar with a programming language like JavaScript or Java, understanding PHP code will be a piece of cake.

Tools

We will use a free code editor called Brackets to create our project from start to finish. To test and visualize the theme, we will use the

XAMPP program, which is a practical local WP server for Windows, Linux, and Mac.

Structure

A WordPress theme is a set of files in PHP format that can contain PHP, HTML, and CSS code. Generally, each important part of a theme has its file so that you can easily edit a specific aspect of the project, in addition to allowing the code to be reused without having to rewrite it.

Important Considerations

Examples and image editing aren't covered in this book, and we also will not explore the visual aspect. The focus here will be only on the code. The person who takes care of the visual identity of any application is the designer.

It is also important to say that this book isn't a PHP course, so you will need to learn to use Google a lot to achieve the desired goal. I also don't program in PHP, only in JavaScript, but I could build the theme used in this book professionally and with advanced features. No programmer knows how to do everything he needs, but it is essential to know how to find answers to our problems in the various sources available on the internet.

Downloading the Valhalla Theme

The Valhalla theme, which I created, serves as our example in this book. To ease your study, I recommend you download it to better analyze the code on your computer.

https://tinyurl.com/valhalla-wp-theme

The password to open the ZIP file is on page 90.

Google as a Work Tool

As a developer, Google will be your best friend. Whenever you are in doubt about how to do something, organize the idea in a brief sentence without prepositions, and search it on Google. The chances you will find a ready-made solution or the way to reach it are very high. Once, I was developing a project in JS, and I needed to mix data completely randomly, but I had no idea how to achieve this. In just a few minutes, I found the code in a programming forum and adapted it to my needs.

CHAPTER 2

Development Environment

Installing the tools

Through the links below, download and install the Brackets editor and the XAMPP server. If this is your first time using these two programs, quickly read the main points of their respective manuals available on their websites.

http://brackets.io
https://www.apachefriends.org

Directories

Our project will have several folders for efficient file organization. Start by creating the main folder and name it as you wish. In our case, the folder is called Valhalla — my theme name. Within this folder, create the subfolders css, images, inc, js, template-parts, and lang.

My recommendation is that you develop your project directly from the WP installation folder so that you can view any changes in your browser. That is why you should use XAMPP or another local server. But you can only install and preview your theme after you created the two required files that will be covered in the next topic.

Main Files

Index.php (required)

This is a required file that WP uses for displaying posts when the home.php file isn't found. In our case, it doesn't contain much code. Let's start by opening our work tool, Brackets. Within the program, click File and then New to create a new file. We will save it inside the main folder by clicking on File and Save. It is very important that you save it with the name index.php.

This is the file contents:

```php
<?php
/*
 * The main template file.
 * @package Valhalla
 * @subpackage Templates
 */

// Do not allow directly accessing this file.

if ( ! defined( 'ABSPATH' ) ) {
exit( 'Direct script access denied.' );
```

```
} ?>

<?php get_header();
get_template_part( 'template-parts/blog-template' );
?>
```

Any PHP code must always be inside the opening <?php and closing ?> tags. Always remember this rule, or your theme won't work.

Any text that is only for informational purposes must go within /* and */; otherwise, the text will be displayed on the page. /* Here is a text visible only to me. */

It is not a rule and changes nothing in the functioning of the theme, but it is interesting to put at the top of the file the information that identifies it. / * The main template file */

The first piece of code, "if (! defined", prevents direct access to the file. This is a security tool, as it makes it impossible for anyone to have access to information they shouldn't have and use it to attack the website, bypass the authentication system, etc.

get_header() - it requests the main site header — header.php — that we will create later.

get_template_part() - it is a function that loads a template part into a template. For example, if you create a sidebar.php template, you can use this function to include it on any page you want it to be displayed.

Don't forget that every function must be closed with a semicolon.

Style.css (required)

In this file, you will put almost all the styles used on the website, but you can create other style sheets if necessary. It is a good practice to organize this file by sections, especially if the theme is for professional use. See an example below:

```
/*
Theme Name: Valhalla
Theme URI: --
Author: Pierre Macedo
Author URI: --
Description: Valhalla is a modern, fast, and highly customizable WordPress theme. It's carefully built under the most modern web design techniques to deliver a great layout with a fresh look to your business website. It differs from other themes, not only aesthetically but also in the way it was coded. It doesn't come with unnecessary scripts or plugins. Our polished code will make your webpages load faster, which is a requisite to improve your business Google rankings. Valhalla also stands out for its customization options. Through the WordPress Theme Customizer, you have access to more than 180 color scheme options, and you can also change fonts, sizes, and alignments. For those with some knowledge in HTML, our theme also offers the possibility to insert arbitrary HTML code in some key areas. Valhalla is also fully
```

responsive, which means it's capable of displaying content nicely on any screen size.

Version: 1.2

License: GNU General Public License v3.0

License URI: https://www.gnu.org/licenses/gpl-3.0.html

Text Domain: valhalla

*/

/*--

>>> TABLE OF CONTENTS:

1.0 - General

2.0 - Menu Bar

3.0 - Home Page Header

4.0 - Home Page

5.0 - About Us Page Header

6.0 - About Us Page

7.0 - Portfolio Page Header

8.0 - Portfolio Page

9.0 - Service Page Header

10 - Service Page

11 - FAQ Page Header

12 - FAQ Page

13 - Contact Page Header

```
14 - Contact Page
15 - Blog Page Header
16 - Blog Page
17 - Post Page Header
18 - Post Page
19 - Comments Template
20 - Other Pages Header
21 - Other Pages
22 - Search Page
23 - Category and Archive Pages
24 - 404 Page
25 - Footer
26 - jQuery UI Tabs
27 - WordPress Core Widgets
28 - HTML Tags and Formatting
29 - Alignment
30 - Gutenberg blocks
------------------------------------------------------------*/
```

Include at the top of the file at least the theme name, author, description, version, and text domain.

Home.php

This is the template for displaying posts. Don't forget that although we can use WP for a website that doesn't have posts, the main function of this platform is to display dynamic content.

```php
<?php
/*
 * The default template for displaying posts.
 * @package Valhalla
 * @subpackage Templates
 */

// Do not allow directly accessing this file.

if ( ! defined( 'ABSPATH' ) ) {
exit( 'Direct script access denied.' );
} ?>

<?php get_header('2');
get_template_part( 'template-parts/blog-template' );
?>
```

Note that the get_header() function now has the argument '2' inside it. This means that the header-2 file will be incorporated. If the argument was '3', the file loaded by WP would be header-3.php and so on.

Front-page.php

This file allows you to configure a static page, without posts, to be the main page of the site. This option is in the WP settings.

```php
<?php
/*
* The Static Front Page template.
* @package Valhalla
* @subpackage Templates
*/

// Do not allow directly accessing this file.

if ( ! defined( 'ABSPATH' ) ) {
exit( 'Direct script access denied.' );
} ?>

<?php
if ( is_front_page() && is_home() ) {
get_header();
get_template_part( 'template-parts/blog-template' );
} elseif ( is_front_page() ) {
get_template_part( 'template-parts/home-template' );
}
?>
```

We use is_front_page() && is_home() to check if the main page of the website is also the page for displaying posts, and if that's the case, we will request the default header and blog template. But if this condition isn't true, and the main page isn't a blog page (elseif), we will use the home page template.

If you don't program in any language, you may be lost as to how the previous code works, but what is happening is that we start an if condition followed by opening and closing parentheses, putting the proper functions inside it; opening bracket followed by the code that will run if our condition is true; closing bracket and the second elseif condition that follows the same patterns as the first.

Note that a space separates each element within our function. This is important to keep the code organized. Also, don't forget that, just like in HTML, everything we open in PHP must be closed. An open parenthesis or bracket is enough to prevent the entire site from working.

Header.php

You have already been introduced to this file on the previous pages. Here we will simply create the top of our theme where images, menu bar, logo, etc., can be displayed. It is possible to have a different header for each page of the site.

```php
<?php
/*
* The header for the home page.
* @package Valhalla
```

```
 * @subpackage Templates
 */

// Do not allow directly accessing this file.

if ( ! defined( 'ABSPATH' ) ) {
exit( 'Direct script access denied.' );
} ?>

<!DOCTYPE html>
<html <?php language_attributes(); ?> class="no-js no-svg">

<head>
<meta charset="<?php bloginfo( 'charset' ); ?>">
<meta name="viewport" content="width=device-width, initial-scale=1">
<link rel="profile" href="https://gmpg.org/xfn/11">
<?php wp_head(); ?>
</head>

<body <?php body_class(); ?>>

<div class="home-header-top-bar-bg">
<div class="home-header-top-bar">
```

```
<i id="header-phone" class="fas fa-lg fa-phone"></i><span
class="phone-top">
<?php echo esc_html( get_theme_mod( 'valhalla_header_phone' ) );
?></span><a href="<?php echo esc_url( get_theme_mod(
'valhalla_header_twitter') ); ?>">
<i id="header-twitter" class="fa fa-lg fa-twitter"></i></a><a
href="<?php echo esc_url( get_theme_mod(
'valhalla_header_facebook') ); ?>">
<i id="header-facebook" class="fa fa-lg fa-facebook-f"></i></a><a
href="<?php echo esc_url( get_theme_mod(
'valhalla_header_instagram') ); ?>">
<i id="header-instagram" class="fa fa-lg fa-instagram"></i></a>
</div>
</div>

<div id="home-header" class="home-header-background1">
<div class="container-fluid home-header-main-div">
<div class="row">
<div class="col">
<?php get_template_part( 'template-parts/header-menu' ); ?>
</div>
</div>
<div class="row">
<div class="col">
<div class="home-header-transparency-image">
```

```php
<img src="<?php echo get_template_directory_uri();
?>/images/transparency.png" alt="<?php esc_attr__('transparent
image', 'valhalla'); ?>" class="img-fluid">
<div class="home-header-headlines">
<div id="header-carousel" class="carousel" data-ride="carousel">
<?php if ( get_theme_mod( 'valhalla_header_headlines') ) {
$settings = get_theme_mod( 'valhalla_header_headlines');
$headlines = count($settings);
$indicator = 0;
$item = 0;
} ?>
<?php if ( $headlines > 1 ) : ?>
<ol class="carousel-indicators">
<?php foreach( $settings as $setting ) : ?>
<li id="indicator<?php echo esc_attr( $indicator ); ?>" data-
target="#header-carousel" data-slide-to="<?php echo esc_attr(
$indicator ); ?>"></li>
<?php $indicator = $indicator + 1; ?>
<?php endforeach; ?>
</ol>
<div class="carousel-inner">
<?php foreach( $settings as $setting ) : ?>
<?php $item = $item + 1; ?>
<div id="carousel-item<?php echo esc_attr( $item ); ?>"
class="carousel-item">
```

```php
<div>
<h1 class="h1-header-headline">
<?php echo esc_html( $setting['field1'] ); ?>
</h1>
<p class="header-carousel-caption">
<?php echo esc_html( $setting['field2'] ); ?>
</p>
</div>
</div>
<?php endforeach; ?>
</div>
<?php else : ?>
<div class="carousel-inner">
<?php foreach( (array) $settings as $setting ) : ?>
<div class="item active">
<div>
<h1 class="h1-header-headline">
<?php echo esc_html( $setting['field1'] ); ?>
</h1>
<p class="header-carousel-caption">
<?php echo esc_html( $setting['field2'] ); ?>
</p>
</div>
</div>
<?php endforeach; ?>
```

```
</div>
<?php endif; ?>
</div>
</div>
</div>
</div>
</div>
</div>
</div>
```

Our header.php file is basically HTML, and we won't go into details about that. We will focus only on the PHP part, as well as in the whole book.

language_attributes() - it adds the language attributes inside the <html> tag.

bloginfo() - it displays site information, such as name, description, etc.

wp_head() - it is a hook that cannot be forgotten and must be included inside the <head> tag. It is through this hook that WP and the plugins used in the theme will include scripts and CSS styles in the header.

body_class() - this function adds CSS classes in the <body> element that can be customized in the style sheet. To do this, just use the inspector tool from any browser and check which classes are being displayed. It is also possible to use different styles depending on the page, being necessary to add a function in the functions.php file. More information can be found at the following link:

https://developer.wordpress.org/reference/functions/body_class/

echo - this function displays the information part of a string. To display any text in PHP code, for example, we would do something like this: echo "Hello".

esc_html() - the theme security is important and, in this respect, we use this function to prevent the text returned from the database and which may contain HTML characters, from being displayed as HTML on the page, which could cause unwanted behavior in our code or be a bridge to various types of attacks.

esc_url() - it follows the same principle as the previous function, but it is used with links.

esc_attr() - at this point, you already know what esc functions are for, and this one is used with attributes, such as "title," "alt," etc.

get_theme_mod() - this is where the possibility of customizing our theme through a panel comes in. You will understand more about this later, but basically, this function returns a value that can be changed by the theme user.

get_template_directory_uri() - very useful for accessing an image or file located in the theme directory. Instead of providing a direct link to the file, with this function, we just need to add the necessary subdirectories.

In the last part of the code there is a custom PHP function to handle the display of different images in the header. It isn't important to explain how it works, as it isn't part of WP. When you start working on your projects, different and customized functions will be required.

So far, you can see that, unlike static websites, WP themes display information through functions, without having to directly write texts, links, etc., in the code.

Note that the <html> and <body> tags were opened in the header but were not closed. This is because the header is just the top of the site. The closing of these two tags is done in the footer file.

Footer.php

If the header displays the upper part of our website, the footer displays the lower part.

```php
<?php
/*
* The template for displaying the footer.
* @package Valhalla
```

```
* @subpackage Templates
*/

// Do not allow directly accessing this file.

if ( ! defined( 'ABSPATH' ) ) {
exit( 'Direct script access denied.' );
}  ?>

<?php wp_footer(); ?>

<div class="container-fluid footer">

<div class="container-fluid footer-main-div">
<div class="container-fluid section-footer">
<div class="row">
<div id="footer-about" class="col-md">
<p class="footer-headings">
<?php echo esc_html( get_theme_mod(
'valhalla_footer_about_heading') ); ?>
</p>
<p class="footer-text">
<?php echo esc_html( get_theme_mod( 'valhalla_footer_about_text')
); ?>
</p>
```

```
</div>
<div id="footer-contact" class="col-md">
<p class="footer-headings">
<?php echo esc_html( get_theme_mod(
'valhalla_footer_contact_heading') ); ?>
</p>
<p class="footer-text"><i id="footer-phone" class="fas fa-lg fa-
phone footer-icons"></i>
<?php echo esc_html( get_theme_mod(
'valhalla_footer_contact_phone') ); ?>
</p>
<p class="footer-text"><i id="footer-whatsapp" class="fa fa-lg fa-
whatsapp footer-icons"></i>
<?php echo esc_html( get_theme_mod(
'valhalla_footer_contact_whatsapp') ); ?>
</p>
<p class="footer-text"><i id="footer-email" class="fa fa-lg fa-at
footer-icons"></i>
<?php echo esc_html( get_theme_mod(
'valhalla_footer_contact_email') ); ?>
</p>
<p class="footer-text"><i id="footer-address" class="fa fa-lg fa-
location-arrow footer-icons"></i>
<?php echo esc_html( get_theme_mod(
'valhalla_footer_contact_address') ); ?>
```

```
</p>
</div>
<div id="footer-social" class="col-md">
<p class="footer-headings">
<?php echo esc_html( get_theme_mod(
'valhalla_footer_social_heading') ); ?>
</p>
<p class="footer-text"><a href="<?php echo esc_url(
get_theme_mod( 'valhalla_footer_social_twitter') ); ?>"><i
id="footer-twitter" class="fa fa-lg fa-twitter footer-
icons"></i> Twitter</a></p>
<p class="footer-text"><a href="<?php echo esc_url(
get_theme_mod( 'valhalla_footer_social_facebook') ); ?>"><i
id="footer-facebook" class="fa fa-lg fa-facebook footer-
icons"></i> Facebook</a></p>
<p class="footer-text"><a href="<?php echo esc_url(
get_theme_mod( 'valhalla_footer_social_instagram') ); ?>"><i
id="footer-instagram" class="fa fa-lg fa-instagram footer-
icons"></i> Instagram</a></p>
</div>
<?php if (is_active_sidebar('sidebar-2')) : ?>
<div id="footer-widget" class="col-md">
<div class="footer-sidebar">
<div id="sidebar">
<ul>
```

```php
<?php dynamic_sidebar('sidebar-2'); ?>
</ul>
</div>
</div>
</div>
<?php endif; ?>
</div>
</div>
</div>

</div>

<div class="container-fluid footer2">
<div class="container-fluid section-footer">
<p>&copy;Copyright 2020  |  Valhalla
Theme <?php echo esc_html__('by', 'valhalla'); ?> Pierre
Macedo  |  <?php echo esc_html__('All
Rights Reserved', 'valhalla'); ?>
</p>
</div>
</div>

</body>

</html>
```

wp_footer() - a hook used to include scripts, styles, and other information that can be added at the bottom of the page. Remember that any script added to the footer is loaded last, so if any part of your theme needs a script right at the beginning of the page loading, then it must be included in the header. But the rule is clear: for better performance, everything that can go in the footer must be placed there.

is_active_sidebar() - in this function, we are checking if there is a menu called sidebar-2 that will display useful links in the footer. Sidebars registration is made in the functions.php file.

dynamic_sidebar() - it is used to display the sidebar or, in this specific case, the footer menu.

404.php

The 404 error page tells website visitors that a requested page doesn't exist.

```php
<?php
/*
 * The 404 error page template.
 * @package Valhalla
 * @subpackage Templates
 */

// Do not allow directly accessing this file.
```

```
if ( ! defined( 'ABSPATH' ) ) {
exit( 'Direct script access denied.' );
} ?>


<?php get_header(); ?>


<div class="main-content-area">


<div class="container-fluid">
<?php get_template_part( 'template-parts/404-template' ); ?>
</div>


</div>


<?php get_footer(); ?>
```

Functions.php

We're entering a crucial part of the theme — the file that contains all the functions for global use. Any error here causes a general error in the installation of WP, making it necessary to access the file directly through the hosting control panel to fix it or upload the fixed file.

```php
<?php
/*
 * Valhalla functions and definitions.
 * @package Valhalla
 * @subpackage Core
 */

// Do not allow directly accessing this file.

if ( ! defined( 'ABSPATH' ) ) {
exit( 'Direct script access denied.' );
}

require_once( dirname( __FILE__ ) . '/inc/class-tgm-plugin-
activation.php' );
require( dirname( __FILE__ ) . '/inc/kirki/kirki.php' );
require( dirname( __FILE__ ) . '/inc/customizer.php' );
require( 'dynamic-styles.php' );

/*
 * Register Custom Navigation Walker
 */

require_once('class-wp-bootstrap-navwalker.php');
```

```php
function valhalla_bootstrap_nav() {
wp_nav_menu( array(
'theme_location'  => 'header-menu',
'depth'         => 2,
'container'     => 'false',
'menu_class'     => 'nav navbar-nav',
'fallback_cb'    => 'wp_bootstrap_navwalker::fallback',
'walker'        => new wp_bootstrap_navwalker())
);
}


function valhalla_register_header_menu() {
register_nav_menu('header-menu',__( 'Header Menu', 'valhalla' ));
}
add_action( 'init', 'valhalla_register_header_menu' );

/*
* Theme setup
*/

function valhalla_setup() {
add_theme_support( 'title-tag' );
add_theme_support( 'automatic-feed-links' );
add_theme_support( 'post-thumbnails' );
add_theme_support( 'wp-block-styles' );
```

```
add_theme_support( 'align-wide' );
add_theme_support( 'align-full' );
add_theme_support( 'editor-styles' );
add_editor_style( 'style-editor.css' );
}
add_action( 'after_setup_theme', 'valhalla_setup' );

/*
* Register sidebars
*/

function valhalla_widgets_init() {
register_sidebar( array(
'name'      => __( 'Left Sidebar', 'valhalla' ),
'id'        => 'sidebar-1',
'description'  => __( 'Add widgets here to appear in the sidebar on
blog posts.', 'valhalla' ),
'before_widget' => '<section id="%1$s" class="widget %2$s">',
'after_widget' => '</section>',
'before_title' => '<h2 class="widget-title">',
'after_title'  => '</h2>',
) );
register_sidebar( array(
'name'      => __( 'Footer Sidebar', 'valhalla' ),
'id'        => 'sidebar-2',
```

```php
'description'  => __( 'Add widgets here to appear in the footer.',
'valhalla' ),
'before_widget' => '<section id="%1$s" class="widget %2$s">',
'after_widget' => '</section>',
'before_title' => '<h2 class="widget-title">',
'after_title' => '</h2>',
) );
}
add_action( 'widgets_init', 'valhalla_widgets_init' );


/*
 * Enqueue scripts and fonts
 */

function valhalla_scripts() {
global $template;
$template_slug = basename( $template );

if ( (is_front_page() && is_home()) || ('index.php' ===
$template_slug) || (is_404())) {
wp_enqueue_script('jquery');
wp_enqueue_script('bootstrap-js', get_template_directory_uri() .
'/js/bootstrap.js', array('jquery'), '4.2.1', true);
```

```
wp_enqueue_script('valhalla-carousel',
get_template_directory_uri() . '/js/valhalla-carousel.js',
array('jquery'), null, true);
}
else if ( is_home()) {
wp_enqueue_script('jquery');
wp_enqueue_script('bootstrap-js', get_template_directory_uri() .
'/js/bootstrap.js', array('jquery'), '4.2.1', true);
}
else if ( is_front_page() || is_page_template('services.php')){
wp_enqueue_script('jquery');
wp_enqueue_script('bootstrap-js', get_template_directory_uri() .
'/js/bootstrap.js', array('jquery'), '4.2.1', true);
wp_enqueue_script('jquery-ui-core');
wp_enqueue_script('jquery-ui-tabs');
wp_enqueue_script('valhalla-carousel',
get_template_directory_uri() . '/js/valhalla-carousel.js',
array('jquery'), null, true);
wp_enqueue_script('font-awesome-shims',
get_template_directory_uri() . '/js/v4-shims.js', array(), '5.0.3', true);
wp_enqueue_script('valhalla-tabs', get_template_directory_uri() .
'/js/valhalla-tabs.js', array(), null, true);
} else {
wp_enqueue_script('jquery');
```

```
wp_enqueue_script('bootstrap-js', get_template_directory_uri() .
'/js/bootstrap.js', array('jquery'), '4.2.1', true);
wp_enqueue_script('font-awesome-shims',
get_template_directory_uri() . '/js/v4-shims.js', array(), '5.0.3', true);
}
}
add_action('wp_enqueue_scripts', 'valhalla_scripts');


function valhalla_footer_scripts() {
if (is_page_template('faq.php')) {
?>
<script>
( function( $ ) {
"use strict";
$( "#faq-button1" ).attr( "aria-expanded", "true" );
$( "#faq-collapse1" ).addClass( "show");
} )(jQuery);
</script>
<?php
}
}
add_action('wp_footer', 'valhalla_footer_scripts');


function valhalla_fonts() {
```

```
wp_enqueue_style( 'google-font-sans-pro',
'https://fonts.googleapis.com/css?family=Source+Sans+Pro', false );
wp_enqueue_style( 'google-font-montserrat',
'https://fonts.googleapis.com/css?family=Montserrat', false );
wp_enqueue_style( 'google-font-libre-baskerville',
'https://fonts.googleapis.com/css?family=Libre+Baskerville', false );
wp_enqueue_style( 'font-awesome',
'https://use.fontawesome.com/releases/v5.7.1/css/all.css', array(),
'5.7.1', false );
}
add_action( 'wp_enqueue_scripts', 'valhalla_fonts' );


/*
* Set content max width
*/


if ( ! isset( $content_width ) ) $content_width = 600;


/*
* Style tags
*/


function valhalla_the_tags($html) {
$postid = get_the_ID();
```

```
$html = str_replace('<a','<a class="badge badge-primary tags-
badge"',$html);
return $html;
}
add_filter('the_tags','valhalla_the_tags',10,1);


/*
* Customizer custom styles
*/

function valhala_customizer_style( $config ) {
return wp_parse_args( array(
'description' => esc_html__( 'Valhalla is a modern, fast and highly
customizable WordPress theme.', 'valhalla' ),
'color_accent' => '#0091EA',
'color_back'   => '#5a6268',
), $config );
}
add_filter( 'kirki_config', 'valhala_customizer_style' );

function valhalla_customizer_additional_style() {
wp_register_style( 'custom_wp_admin_css',
get_template_directory_uri() . '/css/customizer.css', false);
wp_enqueue_style( 'custom_wp_admin_css' );
}
```

```
add_action('admin_enqueue_scripts',
'valhalla_customizer_additional_style');

/*
* Recommend the installation of the Valhalla Contact Form plugin
*/

function valhalla_register_required_plugins() {
$plugins = array(
array(
'name'          => 'Valhalla Contact Form',
'slug'          => 'valhalla-contact-form',
'source'        => get_template_directory() . '/plugins/valhalla-
contact-form.zip',
'required'      => false,
'version'       => '1.0',
'force_activation'  => false,
'force_deactivation' => false,
'external_url'    => '',
'is_callable'     => '',
),
);
$config = array(
'id'        => 'valhalla',
'default_path' => '',
```

```
'menu'     => 'tgmpa-install-plugins',
'has_notices' => true,
'dismissable' => true,
'dismiss_msg' => '',
'is_automatic' => false,
'message'    => '',
);


tgmpa( $plugins, $config );
}
add_action( 'tgmpa_register', 'valhalla_register_required_plugins' );


/*
* Categories widget with hierarchy enabled
*/


function categories_widget_border() {
if (is_single()) {
?>
<script>
( function( $ ) {
"use strict";
$( "ul.children" ).parent().css( "border", "none" );
} )(jQuery);
</script>
```

```php
<?php
}

}
add_action('wp_footer', 'categories_widget_border');
```

Our file contains all functions suitable for the Valhalla theme. I recommend that you don't try to understand how they work, but only what they are for. Use this project code as a template for your future projects. It is very easy to adapt a piece of code to our needs.

require_once(), require() - both can include files; the only difference is that the first one checks if the file has already been included and if so, it won't include it again. In the example given, we are including a plugin activator, a plugin we need to create customizable fields, and the file itself containing the customizations.

dirname() - it returns the site root directory. Again, I recommend that you take the example provided and adapt it for your project by changing the directories and file names.

For the construction of the Valhalla theme menu, I used WP Bootstrap Navwalker. More information at the following link:

https://github.com/wp-bootstrap/wp-bootstrap-navwalker

register_nav_menu() - after accessing the previous link and learning how to build the menu using the wp_nav_menu() function, it is time to register the menu with this function.

add_action() - you must have noticed that at the end of each function, this other one appears. It hooks the function to its action. Two arguments are required within it, which are the hook to which the function is linked and the name of the function itself. You have already been introduced to two hooks in this book - wp_head and wp_footer. If we create the valhalla_footer_scripts() function to include scripts in the footer, our add_action() will look like this:

```
add_action('wp_footer', 'valhalla_footer_scripts');
```

wp_enqueue_script() - it adds scripts to our theme. This function has several arguments. In our example, we use array() to indicate the script dependency; that is, I need jQuery to be loaded before Bootstrap because Bootstrap has features that are dependent on it. The other two arguments are the script version and true. The "true" argument authorizes the script to be loaded in the footer. If you need to load it in the header, use false. Note that WP already has a built-in version of jQuery, so you don't need to indicate any JS file in this case.

In our valhalla_scripts() function, we use conditionals to check which page is displayed and thus include only the necessary scripts for that page. This improves performance since the scripts will be loaded only where they are requested.

wp_register_style() - it is a function used to register style sheets, but it is only necessary when we want to avoid conflicts between any plugin and our theme. Otherwise, it is optional.

wp_enqueue_style() - it is used to include the style sheets and Google fonts used in the theme.

admin_enqueue_scripts() - as the Valhalla theme has a panel where users can customize texts, colors, images, etc., we use this hook to add style sheets to the WP admin area so that we can style the administration panel to suit the theme proposal. To make it clear, any visual modification you want to make in the restricted area of WP, you'll need to add it to a style sheet used exclusively to modify that area.

add_theme_support() - it adds features to the theme, for example, Editor Style allows you to use a style sheet to modify the appearance of the WP content editor.

register_sidebar() - just as we need to register the navigation menu, we also need to register the side menu or sidebar if our theme has one. Despite the name "side," this function is also used to register the menu that appears in the footer. The sidebars will appear in the WP Widgets section with the names in which they were registered in functions.php. With this, theme users can add several widgets to any sidebars, and they will be automatically displayed on the website.

Secondary Files

Category.php

If you are developing a professional theme, your client may also want to use his website for a blog. Therefore, it is interesting to have a page that displays all posts organized by categories.

```php
<?php
/*
* The template for displaying category pages.
* @package Valhalla
* @subpackage Templates
*/

// Do not allow directly accessing this file.

if ( ! defined( 'ABSPATH' ) ) {
exit( 'Direct script access denied.' );
} ?>

<?php get_header('2'); ?>

<div class="main-content-area">

<div class="container-fluid widget-page-section1">
```

```php
<?php if ( have_posts() ) : ?>
<?php while ( have_posts() ) : the_post(); ?>
<div class="card mb-3">
<div class="card-body">
<h5 class="card-title"><a href="<?php the_permalink() ?>"
rel="bookmark" title="<?php printf(__('Permanent Link to %s',
'valhalla'), the_title_attribute()) ?>">
<?php the_title(); ?></a></h5>
<small>
<?php the_time(__('F j, Y', 'valhalla')) ?>
<?php echo esc_html__(' by ', 'valhalla'); ?>
<?php the_author_posts_link() ?></small>
<?php the_excerpt(); ?>
<p class="postmetadata">
<?php comments_popup_link(__('No comments yet', 'valhalla'), __('1
comment', 'valhalla'), __('% comments', 'valhalla'), 'comments-link',
__('Comments closed','valhalla')); ?>
</p>
</div>
</div>
<?php endwhile; ?>
<div class="pages-navigation">
<?php echo wp_kses_post(paginate_links()); ?>
</div>
<?php else: ?>
```

```php
<?php get_template_part( 'template-parts/404-template' ); ?>
<?php endif; ?>
</div>

<div class="content-separator"></div>

</div>
<?php get_footer(); ?>
```

This code contains a function that checks if there are any posts to be displayed and extracts some information from these posts, such as the link the_permalink() and the title the_title().

Note the "while (have_posts())" line, it tells the code that while there are posts to show, generate a <div> for each post. And we close our "while" function immediately after the last </div> that closes the main <div>.

wp_kses_post() - it filters the HTML allowed in the posts area.

paginate_links() - it creates pagination if posts need to be displayed on more than one page.

The function continues with an "else" in case there are no posts, and then the 404 error page is shown and ends right after with endif.

The sample code displays a list of posts when the user clicks on a category. To display a list of categories, the theme user must add the corresponding widget in the WP panel. In the Valhalla theme, the two areas where the Categories Widget can be added are the sidebar and the footer menu.

Archive.php

A page to show all posts separated by month, year, subject, etc.

```php
<?php
/*
* The template for displaying archive pages.
* @package Valhalla
* @subpackage Templates
*/

// Do not allow directly accessing this file.

if ( ! defined( 'ABSPATH' ) ) {
exit( 'Direct script access denied.' );
} ?>

<?php get_header('2'); ?>

<div class="main-content-area">

<div class="container-fluid widget-page-section1">
<div class="search-page-form">
```

```php
<?php get_search_form(); ?>
</div>
<?php if (have_posts()) : while (have_posts()) : the_post(); ?>
<div class="card mb-3">
<div class="card-body">
<h5 class="card-title"><a href="<?php the_permalink(); ?>">
<?php the_title(); ?></a></h5>
<p class="card-text">
<?php the_excerpt(); ?>
</p>
</div>
</div>
<?php endwhile; ?>
<div class="pages-navigation">
<?php echo wp_kses_post(paginate_links()); ?>
</div>
<?php else : ?>
<?php get_template_part( 'template-parts/404-template' ); ?>
<?php endif; ?>
</div>

<div class="content-separator"></div>

</div>
<?php get_footer(); ?>
```

get_search_form() - it displays the search form.

The sample code displays a list of posts when the user clicks on an archive. To display a list of archives, the theme user must add the corresponding widget in the WP panel. In the Valhalla theme, the two areas where the Archives Widget can be added are the sidebar and the footer menu.

Comments.php

Template for displaying comments on posts.

```php
<?php
/*
* The template for displaying comments.
* @package Valhalla
* @subpackage Templates
*/

// Do not allow directly accessing this file.

if ( ! defined( 'ABSPATH' ) ) {
exit( 'Direct script access denied.' );
} ?>

<div id="comments" class="comments-area">
```

```php
<?php if ( have_comments() ) : ?>
<h4 class="comments-title">
<?php echo esc_html__( 'Comments', 'valhalla' ); ?>
</h4>
<?php if ( get_comment_pages_count() > 1 && get_option(
'page_comments' ) ) : ?>
<nav id="comment-nav-above" class="navigation comment-
navigation" role="navigation">
<h5 class="screen-reader-text">
<?php echo esc_html__( 'Comment navigation', 'valhalla' ); ?>
</h5>
<div class="nav-previous">
<?php previous_comments_link( esc_html__( 'Older Comments',
'valhalla' ) ); ?>
</div>
<div class="nav-next">
<?php next_comments_link( esc_html__( 'Newer Comments',
'valhalla' ) ); ?>
</div>
</nav>
<?php endif; ?>
<ol class="comment-list">
<?php
wp_list_comments( array(
'style'    => 'ol',
```

```php
'short_ping' => true,
'avatar_size'=> 34,
));
?>
</ol>
<?php if ( get_comment_pages_count() > 1 && get_option(
'page_comments' ) ) : ?>
<nav id="comment-nav-above" class="navigation comment-
navigation" role="navigation">
<h5 class="screen-reader-text">
<?php echo esc_html__( 'Comment navigation', 'valhalla' ); ?>
</h5>
<div class="nav-previous">
<?php previous_comments_link( esc_html__( 'Older Comments',
'valhalla' ) ); ?>
</div>
<div class="nav-next">
<?php next_comments_link( esc_html__( 'Newer Comments',
'valhalla' ) ); ?>
</div>
</nav>
<?php endif; ?>
<?php if ( ! comments_open() ) : ?>
<p class="no-comments">
<?php echo esc_html__( 'Comments are closed.', 'valhalla' ); ?>
```

```
</p>
<?php endif; ?>
<?php endif; ?>


<?php comment_form(); ?>


</div>
```

This code is quite simple to understand, and the functions have obvious names. What the code is doing is simply checking for any comments to display.

get_comment_pages_count() - it returns the number of pages in the comments area, that is, comments that have pagination.

get_option() - a function used to return option values that are settings and preferences stored in WP. In our case, we use the page_comments option to check whether comments are paginated.

Searchform.php

Let's create the theme search form.

```php
<?php
/*
* The template for displaying the search form.
* @package Valhalla
* @subpackage Templates
```

```php
*/

// Do not allow directly accessing this file.

if ( ! defined( 'ABSPATH' ) ) {
exit( 'Direct script access denied.' );
} ?>

<form action="<?php echo esc_url( home_url( '/' ) ); ?>" method="get"
accept-charset="utf-8" id="searchform" role="search">

<div class="search-form">
<div>
<input class="search-box" type="text" name="s" id="s" value="<?php
the_search_query(); ?>" placeholder="<?php echo esc_html__(
'Search for...', 'valhalla' ); ?>" />
</div>
<button type="submit" class="btn search-button <?php echo
esc_attr( get_theme_mod( 'valhalla_post_search_button_style', 'btn-
secondary' ) ); ?>" id="searchsubmit"><?php echo esc_html__(
'Search', 'valhalla' ); ?></button>
</div>

</form>
```

Quite simple code that you can simply copy to your project, changing only the CSS classes, the form text, text domain, and get_theme_mod.

Search.php

The search results page.

```php
<?php
/*
* The template for displaying search results pages.
* @package Valhalla
* @subpackage Templates
*/

// Do not allow directly accessing this file.

if ( ! defined( 'ABSPATH' ) ) {
exit( 'Direct script access denied.' );
} ?>

<?php get_header('2'); ?>

<div class="main-content-area">

<div class="container-fluid search-section1">
<div class="search-page-form">
```

```php
<?php get_search_form(); ?>
</div>
<?php  if (have_posts()) : while (have_posts()) : the_post(); ?>
<div class="card mb-3">
<div class="card-body">
<h5 class="search-post-title card-title"><a href="<?php
the_permalink(); ?>">
<?php the_title(); ?></a></h5>
<p class="search-post-excerpt card-text">
<?php the_excerpt(); ?>
</p>
</div>
</div>
<?php endwhile; ?>
<div class="pages-navigation">
<?php echo wp_kses_post(paginate_links( $args )); ?>
</div>
<?php else : ?>
<?php get_template_part( 'template-parts/404-template' ); ?>
<?php endif; ?>
</div>

<div class="content-separator"></div>

</div>
```

```php
<?php get_footer(); ?>
```

Code very similar to the category page and very easy to understand. The posts will be displayed according to the text entered in the search form. If no results are found, the standard error page is displayed. You can create a template other than the 404 to display on the search page.

Single.php

Essential file to display posts individually, that is, when someone clicks on a link to a post, this will be the page where the post will be shown.

```php
<?php
/*
* The template for displaying single posts.
* @package Valhalla
* @subpackage Templates
*/

// Do not allow directly accessing this file.

if ( ! defined( 'ABSPATH' ) ) {
exit( 'Direct script access denied.' );
} ?>
```

```php
<?php get_header('2'); ?>

<div class="container-fluid post-main-content-area">

<div class="row post-row">
<?php if (is_active_sidebar('sidebar-1')) : ?>
<div class="col-md-9">
<?php else : ?>
<div class="col-md-12">
<?php endif; ?>
<div class="post-section">
<?php if ( have_posts() ) : while ( have_posts() ) : the_post(); ?>
<?php
$thumb_id = get_post_thumbnail_id(get_the_ID());
$alt = get_post_meta($thumb_id, '_wp_attachment_image_alt',
true);
?>
<div class="post-image-div"><img alt="<?php echo esc_attr( $alt );
?>" class="post-image" src="<?php echo
esc_url(wp_get_attachment_url( get_post_thumbnail_id('') ));
?>"></div>
<div <?php post_class('post-content') ?> id="post-<?php the_ID();
?>">
<?php the_content(''); ?>
```

```php
</div>
<div class="clear-fix"></div>
<p class="post-author">
<?php the_author() ?>
<?php echo esc_html__( ' on ', 'valhalla'); ?>
<?php the_time(__('F j, Y', 'valhalla')) ?>
</p>
<?php if(has_tag()) : ?>
<?php
$tags = get_the_tags(get_the_ID());
foreach($tags as $tag){
echo '<a href="'.esc_url(get_tag_link($tag->term_id)).'" rel="tag"
class="badge badge-primary post-tags-style">'.esc_attr($tag-
>name).'</a> ';
} ?>
<?php endif; ?>
<?php echo wp_kses_post('<div class="post-pagination">');
wp_link_pages( array(
'before'    => wp_kses_post('<div class="post-page-links"><span
class="post-page-links-title">' . __( 'Pages:', 'valhalla' ) . '</span>'),
'after'    => wp_kses_post('</div>'),
'link_before' => wp_kses_post('<span class="no">'),
'link_after' => wp_kses_post('</span>'),
) );
echo wp_kses_post('</div>');
```

```php
?>
<?php if ( comments_open() || get_comments_number() ) :
comments_template();
endif; ?>
<?php endwhile; else: ?>
<?php get_template_part( 'template-parts/404-template' ); ?>
<?php endif; ?>
</div>
</div>
<?php if (is_active_sidebar('sidebar-1')) : ?>
<div class="col-md-3">
<div class="post-sidebar">
<div id="sidebar">
<ul>
<?php dynamic_sidebar('sidebar-1'); ?>
</ul>
</div>
</div>
</div>
<?php endif; ?>
</div>

<div class="content-separator"></div>

</div>
```

```php
<?php get_footer(); ?>
```

is_active_sidebar() - with this function, we check if there is a sidebar named sidebar-1 registered in the functions file. If it exists, we start the code with a column of a certain width; otherwise, we proceed with a different width.

In the piece of code highlighted below, we store the post image ID in the $thumb_id variable. The $alt variable is used to store the image metadata (alt text) through the get_post_meta() function that takes the $thumb_id argument.

```php
<?php
$thumb_id = get_post_thumbnail_id(get_the_ID());
$alt = get_post_meta($thumb_id, '_wp_attachment_image_alt',
true);
?>
```

A variable has the simple function of storing information to be re-used within the same code on the same page. In the example given, the $alt variable is used to fill the alt attribute inside the <img> tag. A variable name is a free choice. But pay attention: a variable must be defined before it is used; otherwise, no information will be displayed.

wp_get_attachment_url(get_post_thumbnail_id('')) - it will return the link to the post image.

post_class() - here we define that post-content will be the CSS class we will use in the posts area.

has_tag() - we use it to check if the post has tags and, if it does, we run a function to display them.

Additional Files

Dynamic-styles.php

The Valhalla theme presented in this book is highly customizable, allowing the user to change all colors on the website. To achieve this level of customization, it is necessary to create dynamic styles. This process can be done directly in the functions file, but it is preferable to create a file for this task and include it in functions.php through the require() function.

The top of the file is the pattern you already know:

```php
<?php
/*
* Valhalla dynamic styles function.
* @package Valhalla
* @subpackage Core
*/

// Do not allow directly accessing this file.
```

```
if ( ! defined( 'ABSPATH' ) ) {
exit( 'Direct script access denied.' );
}
```

All the code goes within a function like this:

```
function valhalla_dynamic_styles() { }
```

We initially check which page is being displayed so that we can include the necessary style sheets and create the dynamic CSS.

To check if the page is index.php, we need to use an additional trick, as shown below:

```
global $template;
$template_slug = basename( $template );
```

This is how we check several pages at the same time, including index.php:

```
if ( ( is_front_page() && is_home()) || (is_front_page()) || (is_404()) ||
('index.php' === $template_slug) ) {
wp_enqueue_style('bootstrap', get_template_directory_uri() .
'/css/bootstrap.css', array(), '4.2.1');
wp_enqueue_style('jquery-ui-theme', get_template_directory_uri()
. '/css/jquery-ui.css');
```

```
wp_enqueue_style('valhalla-style', get_template_directory_uri() .
'/style.css', array('bootstrap', 'jquery-ui-theme'));
wp_enqueue_style('valhalla-style-responsive',
get_template_directory_uri() . '/style-responsive.css',
array('valhalla-style')); }
```

The next step is to add the variables that will store the colors the user has customized in the theme panel:

```
$bg1_color1 = get_theme_mod( 'valhalla_home_header_bg1_color1',
'#131b80');
$bg1_color2 = get_theme_mod( 'valhalla_home_header_bg1_color2',
'#040325');
$bg2_color1 = get_theme_mod( 'valhalla_home_header_bg2_color1',
'#0a5d9f');
$bg2_color2 = get_theme_mod( 'valhalla_home_header_bg2_color2',
'#1e92dd');
$bg3_color1 = get_theme_mod( 'valhalla_home_header_bg3_color1',
'#2f2e34');
$bg3_color2 = get_theme_mod( 'valhalla_home_header_bg3_color2',
'#16151a');
```

The get_theme_mod() function has two arguments. The first accesses the respective information in the database that has the color defined by the user for a specific area of the website. The second is the default color if the color has not yet been changed.

Now we need to perform some other checks according to our theme needs and create the dynamic styles:

```
if ('gradient' == get_theme_mod('valhalla_header_style_home',
'gradient')) {
$header_bg = "
.home-header-background1 {
background: {$bg1_color1} ;
background: -moz-radial-gradient(circle, {$bg1_color1} 0%,
{$bg1_color2} 50%);
background: -webkit-radial-gradient(circle, {$bg1_color1} 0%,
{$bg1_color2} 50%);
background: radial-gradient(circle, {$bg1_color1} 0%, {$bg1_color2}
50%); } ";
wp_add_inline_style( 'valhalla-style', $header_bg ); }
```

In the code above, we store the CSS inside a variable, and the properties are populated using the variables defined at the beginning of the function. Each section must be added to an existing style sheet as in the following example:

```
wp_add_inline_style( 'valhalla-style', $header_bg );
```

wp_add_inline_style() - this function allows you to add extra styles to an already enqueued style sheet. In our case, right after the page verification, we enqueued the valhalla-style style sheet.

Here is a brief example of everything explained in this section:

```
function valhalla_dynamic_styles() {
global $template;
$template_slug = basename( $template );

/* Enqueue styles for the home page */

if ( (is_front_page() && is_home()) || (is_front_page()) || (is_404()) ||
('index.php' === $template_slug) ) {
wp_enqueue_style('valhalla-style', get_template_directory_uri() .
'/style.css', array('bootstrap', 'jquery-ui-theme'));

$bg1_color1 = get_theme_mod( 'valhalla_home_header_bg1_color1',
'#131b80');
$bg1_color2 = get_theme_mod( 'valhalla_home_header_bg1_color2',
'#040325');

if ('gradient' == get_theme_mod('valhalla_header_style_home',
'gradient')) {
$header_bg = "
.home-header-background1 {
background: {$bg1_color1} ;
background: -moz-radial-gradient(circle, {$bg1_color1} 0%,
{$bg1_color2} 50%);
```

```
background: -webkit-radial-gradient(circle, {$bg1_color1} 0%,
{$bg1_color2} 50%); } ";
wp_add_inline_style( 'valhalla-style', $header_bg );  }  }  }
```

Templates

This topic isn't about a specific file but the possibility of creating ready-made templates for any page on the site. The only thing you should know in this regard is that every page template must start with the following line of code:

```
<?php /* Template Name: Contact */ ?>
```

The line above will allow WP to identify such a file as a template. In our example, the name we gave to the template was Contact, but you can name yours as you like.

Although it is possible to force WP to create pages automatically when installing themes, this is not recommended. Therefore, all necessary pages must be created manually in the WP editor, and then we select which template will be used for that page.

Page.php

Your theme users may want to create a personalized page instead of using the ready-made templates. For that, your theme must have the page.php file.

```php
<?php
/*
 * The template for displaying all pages.
 * @package Valhalla
 * @subpackage Templates
 */

// Do not allow directly accessing this file.

if ( ! defined( 'ABSPATH' ) ) {
exit( 'Direct script access denied.' );
} ?>

<?php get_header('2'); ?>

<div class="main-content-area">

<div class="container-fluid page-section1">
<div class="page-content">
<?php while ( have_posts() ) : the_post(); ?>
<?php the_content();?>
<?php endwhile; ?>
</div>
<div class="clear-fix"></div>
<?php if ( comments_open() || get_comments_number() ) :
```

```
comments_template();
endif; ?>
<?php echo wp_kses_post('<div class="pages-navigation">');
wp_link_pages( array(
'before'    => wp_kses_post('<div class="page-links"><span
class="page-links-title">' . __( 'Pages:', 'valhalla' ) . '</span>'),
'after'    => wp_kses_post('</div>'),
'link_before' => wp_kses_post('<span class="no">'),
'link_after' => wp_kses_post('</span>'),
) );
echo wp_kses_post('</div>');
?>
</div>

<div class="content-separator"></div>

</div>

<?php get_footer(); ?>
```

The previous code displays the content entered in the WP page editor. The header, footer, and website structure are the same.

Blank.php

With page.php, the user is limited to creating a page with the standard theme structure. To work around this problem, we create an empty page template that will contain only the footer. If you want to remove the footer, be sure to close the <html> and <body> tags in the file itself.

```php
<?php /* Template Name: Blank */ ?>
<?php
/*
* Blank page template
* @package Valhalla
* @subpackage Templates
*/

// Do not allow directly accessing this file.

if ( ! defined( 'ABSPATH' ) ) {
exit( 'Direct script access denied.' );
}  ?>

<!DOCTYPE html>
<html <?php language_attributes(); ?> class="no-js no-svg">

<head>
<meta charset="<?php bloginfo( 'charset' ); ?>">
<meta name="viewport" content="width=device-width, initial-scale=1">
<link rel="profile" href="https://gmpg.org/xfn/11">
```

```
<?php wp_head(); ?>
</head>

<body <?php body_class(); ?>>

<div class="blank-page-section1">
<?php while ( have_posts() ) : the_post(); ?>
<?php the_content(); ?>
<?php endwhile; ?>
</div>

<div class="content-separator"></div>

<?php get_footer(); ?>
```

Screenshot.png

When your theme is finished, make a 1200x900 pixels screenshot of the home page and save it in the main folder. This image will be displayed in the themes area within WP. This file is mandatory if you intend to upload the theme to the WP directory.

CHAPTER 3

Template Part

You have already been taught that it is possible to reuse a piece of code in more than one file without having to copy and paste the code multiple times. For example, the Valhalla theme has two headers and, instead of pasting the same menu code in both files, we create a template part for the menu and use the following function to include it in both headers:

```php
<?php get_template_part( 'template-parts/header-menu' ); ?>
```

In the code above, template-parts is just the name of the directory where the header-menu.php file is located. Note that it isn't necessary to include the php extension in the file name.

Below is the header-menu.php code:

```php
<?php
/*
* Template part for displaying the header menu.
* @package Valhalla
* @subpackage Templates
*/
```

```php
// Do not allow directly accessing this file.

if ( ! defined( 'ABSPATH' ) ) {
exit( 'Direct script access denied.' );
} ?>

<nav id="header-nav-bar" class="navbar navbar-expand-md
navbar-light <?php if (!get_theme_mod( 'valhalla_header_logo_url'))
: echo " no-logo"; endif; ?>">

<a class="navbar-brand" href="<?php echo esc_url( get_site_url() );
?>">
<?php if ( get_theme_mod( 'valhalla_header_logo_url') ) : ?>
<img src="<?php echo esc_url( get_theme_mod(
'valhalla_header_logo_url') ); ?>" alt="<?php echo
esc_attr(get_bloginfo( 'name' )); ?>" class="img-fluid site-logo">
<?php endif; ?>
</a>

<button class="navbar-toggler ml-auto" type="button" data-
toggle="collapse" data-target="#navbar-content" aria-
controls="navbar-content" aria-expanded="false" aria-label="<?php
echo esc_html__( 'Toggle Navigation', 'valhalla' ); ?>">
```

```
<span class="navbar-custom-toggler-icon"><i class="fas fa-
bars"></i></span>
</button>

<div class="collapse navbar-collapse justify-content-end"
id="navbar-content">
<?php valhalla_bootstrap_nav(); ?>
</div>


</nav>
```

Making the Theme Translatable

In the style.css file, there is a line called Text Domain. This is an argument that allows the translation of texts in the theme. In our case, the text domain is valhalla. Take a look at the piece of code below:

```
esc_html__('All Rights Reserved', 'valhalla')
```

The valhalla argument comes right after the text and is separated by a comma. Any text you want to be translatable must be placed inside the __() function.

First, add the following line to the style.css file below the text domain:

Domain Path: /lang

Add the code below to the functions file replacing valhalla with your text domain:

```
add_action( 'plugins_loaded', function() {
        load_theme_textdomain( 'valhalla', get_template_directory()
. '/lang' ); });
```

1 - Download the Poedit program from the poedit.net website.

2 - Open the program after installation, click File > New.

3 - In the window that opens, type en_US if you want the base language to be the United States English or choose another one from the list.

4 - Click OK.

5 - Go to File > Save as and save the file inside your theme's lang folder. Don't change the file name.

6 - Click Extract from sources.

7 - In the window that opens, click on the + sign and add the root folder of your theme.

8 - Now go to the Sources keywords tab. Click the + button and add one by one of the following keywords:

- __
- _x:1,2c
- _e
- _ex:1,2c
- _n:1,2
- _n_noop:1,2
- _nx:1,2,4c
- _nx_noop:1,2,4c
- esc_attr__
- esc_attr_e
- esc_attr_x:1,2c
- esc_html__
- esc_html_e
- esc_html_x:1,2c

9 - Uncheck the "Also use default keywords for supported languages."

10 - Click OK.

11 - Save the file.

Your theme now has a PO file that can be used to translate the theme into multiple languages. Your clients can use the Loco Translate plugin for this task.

Styling WordPress Widgets

Themes should have at least one area where you can add widgets. Valhalla has the sidebar and menu in the footer. However, widgets are added directly from the WP admin area and have the standard platform style. The developer needs to check which CSS classes are being used in each widget through the browser inspector tool and thus make the necessary changes to the style.css style sheet.

Customizations

WordPress has a panel where you can change some theme options and view the changes made before saving them. Using a framework called Kirki, I added a big list of customizable options to the Valhalla theme panel. The file that has these settings — customizer.php — has almost 5500 lines of code. It was a job that took a few days to complete because, in addition to the time needed to learn how the tool works, I had to make revisions to correct several errors.

Unfortunately, I can't explain how Kirki works, as this would require several pages and increase the level of complexity in this book. I have previously explained everything you need to create a theme. Kirki is something more advanced that requires you to read all the documentation to learn how to use it. On the website kirki.org, many tutorials are available teaching how to use all the features of this tool. But to help you get started, let's see an example:

```
Kirki::add_panel( 'valhalla_header', array(
  'priority'  => 10,
  'title'     => esc_html__( 'Header', 'valhalla' ),
  'description' => esc_html__( '', 'valhalla' ),
));
```

In the previous code, we created a panel called Header within the WP Theme Customizer, where it will contain the settings for the header.

Now we will create a section called Site Logo within the Header panel, which will allow us to change the site logo:

```
Kirki::add_section( 'valhalla_header_logo', array(
    'title'       => esc_html__( 'Site logo', 'valhalla' ),
    'description'  => esc_html__( '', 'valhalla' ),
    'panel'       => 'valhalla_header',
    'priority'    => 160,
));
```

Within the Site Logo section, we will add a field that allows the upload of images:

```
Kirki::add_field( 'valhalla_config', [
        'type'      => 'image',
        'settings'  => 'valhalla_header_logo_url',
        'label'     => esc_html__( 'Upload a logo', 'valhalla' ),
```

```
      'description' => esc_html__( 'Ideally, an image logo should
have equal dimensions, for example, 200x200.', 'valhalla' ),
      'section'   => 'valhalla_header_logo',
      'default'   => '',
] );
```

This is basically how Kirki works with three levels of configuration: panel> section> field or control.

The result is this:

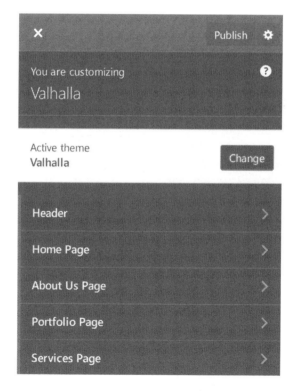

Performance

The speed at which theme pages load depends on several factors. Plugins installed by the user and hosting server are some of them, but we as developers must do our part by keeping our code as clean as possible, without anything unnecessary. It is also important that all scripts that don't need to be loaded before the page code are included in the footer, ensuring that the visual elements of the website load first.

Theme Check

Theme Check is a plugin used to test the theme code and check if all the rules and recommendations of WP itself have been followed. This will ensure that your code works in the best possible way. But keep in mind that not all alerts shown by this plugin represent a risk and need to be changed. Only if you intend to submit your theme to the WordPress directory that you will need to fix 100% of the alerts. In any case, always fix what is considered critical and threatens the security of the theme.

PHP Operators

The symbols in the following table are called operators and are widely used when we want to express a condition to run a function.

&&	And
||	Or
>	Greater than
<	Less than
==	Equal
===	It means identical, verifying not only that the values are equal but that the data type is also the same.
!=	Not equal
!==	Not identical
>=	Greater than or equal to
<=	Less than or equal to
!	Not true

For example, if we want to check if the comments on our website are open, we use the code below:

```
if ( comments_open() )
```

But if we want to know if the comments are not open, we do the following:

```
if ( !comments_open() )
```

That is, we use the exclamation mark (!) to deny the veracity of something in our code.

WordPress.org Rules

To make a theme available for download in the WP directory, an extensive list of rules needs to be followed. I honestly don't think it is worth the effort. The time you would spend studying those rules and applying them to your theme, you could be working on another project. It is very good to develop a project without having to follow a manual with several requirements that are not necessary for the functioning of the website.

CHAPTER 4

Back-End or Front-End?

When you finish reading this book, you will be able to work with the entire visual part of WordPress and use PHP to generate dynamic content, so you are a front-end developer. To become a back-end developer, you need to master the PHP language.

How Much Should I Charge to Develop a Theme?

This depends on the complexity of the project. The most important thing is to not accept proposals that don't value your skills. The amount offered must be enough to cover your working hours. Some clients will offer $200 or less to develop a theme that may take 30 days to complete. This amount doesn't even pay 15 days of work. Don't let anyone exploit you.

What Is a GPL License?

WordPress encourages all themes developed on their platform to be licensed under the GPL. This means that anyone who buys your theme will have the right to modify, distribute it for free, and even sell it. Many developers are uncomfortable with this, and the solution is to use a split license where the PHP and HTML code is under the GPL, but images, CSS, and JavaScript are not.

If I Use the GPL License, How Will I Make Money?

Your theme should be available for download only upon payment, regardless of the license used. You should also add value to the product by offering support and updates only to people who have purchased the theme. It is unlikely a corporate client will use a digital product without guarantees of receiving updates.

APPENDIX

Valhalla: User Manual

The theme that was developed throughout this book is quite complete, and of course, it has a user manual. If you're starting with WordPress and have doubts about themes management, in the manual that is inside the "documentation" folder, you have access to all the instructions for adding pages, setting a static page, adding a menu, etc. There are six topics with detailed explanations of how Valhalla works, which will surely help you with the information you need to provide to your clients.

Useful Links

WordPress functions

https://codex.wordpress.org/Function_Reference

Troubleshooting

https://codex.wordpress.org/Troubleshooting

Theme review guidelines

https://developer.wordpress.org/themes/release/theme-review-guidelines

PHP documentation

https://www.php.net/manual

Password: **38524**

If you encounter any problems in downloading or extracting the ZIP file, send an email to contact@virgopublishers.com, and we will solve it.

Made in the USA
Columbia, SC
23 April 2025

57077618R00050